LOOKING FOR JESUS

Dorothy and Thomas John Carlisle

Looking for Jesus

THOMAS JOHN CARLISLE

William B. Eerdmans Publishing Company
Grand Rapids, Michigan

Copyright © 1993 by Wm. B. Eerdmans Publishing Co.
255 Jefferson Ave. S.E., Grand Rapids, Mich. 49503

Printed in the United States of America

Library of Congress Cataloging-in-Publication Data

Carlisle, Thomas John.
    Looking for Jesus / Thomas John Carlisle.
        p.   cm.
    Includes index.
    ISBN 0-8028-0667-8 (pbk.)
    1. Christian poetry, American.   2. Jesus Christ — Poetry.
    I. Title.
    PS3553.A73L66   1993
    811'.54 — dc20   93-19543
                                                                CIP

THIS BOOK IS DEDICATED

to Ruby Grace Mann Carlisle and Thomas Houston Carlisle, my beloved parents, both of whom made natural in me the love of Jesus and devotion to his service;

to Elizabeth M. Carlisle, my sister;

and to Harold Marten Davis and Mae Marjorie Sanders Davis, who brought up my wife Dorothy to love Jesus too and to be able to share with me more than fifty-four years of marriage and ministry.

CONTENTS

Has Bethlehem Happened to Me?

His Real Humanity

Christ, You Carried a Flower

Poet and Troubadour

Liberation Story

Breath of Life

FOREWORD

> And I heard a voice from heaven saying, "Write
> this: Blessed are the dead who from now on die
> in the Lord."
>
> Revelation 14:13a, NRSV

"Write!" This was one of our father's favorite commands in Scripture, and he did it faithfully and prodigiously. We remember his sitting at isolated picnic tables in the woods beside our favorite lake — writing. We recall his penciling inspirations on file cards in the darkness of the middle of the night, waiting for the daylight the next morning for editing. "Write!" and he did.

On August 17, 1992, the words of the rest of the verse of John also came true for Dad. Called home to God after a heart attack, he was reunited with our mother after nineteen months apart.

We would feel the loss with anguish if it were not for the gain from his life. We have been given words of faith and love and insight into the wonders and mysteries of God's world and the life of Jesus Christ. We are grateful for his faith and his faithfulness. We pray that his words in this twelfth volume of poetry, nearly ready for publication when he died, might nurture and challenge and stimulate your faith in the Lord.

Jesus promises us this: "I came that they may have life, and have it abundantly" (John 10:10, NRSV).

Thomas and Leah Mae
Christopher and Linda
David and Joyce
Jonathan and Susan

(the sons and
daughters-in-love of
Dorothy Mae and
Thomas John Carlisle)

PREFACE

"Looking for Jesus" is the story of my life. I believe that I had some sense of him, first of all, from my mother, perhaps even before I was born. She loved Hoffman's portrayal of the Lord Jesus in the Temple. She also had a picture on our living room wall of Sir Galahad — the knight who went in search of the Holy Grail.

By using this title, I do not mean to imply that Jesus has been absent from my life. My point is that there is always more and more to be found out about him and always more to achieve in identifying him with even partial accuracy.

Among the other titles I might have chosen for this book are *I Call Him Poet, The Living Word, He Comes to Us, Poet and Troubadour, Liberation Story,* or simply *A Commentary* — on the life and words and works and meaning of Jesus Christ. Although this collection is not exhaustive, it does touch on a great many of the episodes contained in the four Gospels.

This book might have been an anthology of poems I gleaned from the hundreds of books I own which contain one or more poems about Jesus. Instead, I have been presumptuous enough to attempt a whole book of poems of my own about Jesus.

In my nearly eighty years of loving poetry both for its own sake and for what it can do for me again and again, Jesus has been my inspiration. In one way or another, he has informed everything I have written. I believe that those poems which have an element of value have been "given" to me. But I have no desire to blame God for those poems that may lack this element. Since I have written about twenty-five hundred poems, fifteen hundred of which have been published, it may seem that my life has been a marathon of writing in which quantity has been my main goal. But this was true only for a short time in my youth. I have written prolifically because I have felt it was essential to write down what came to me — and then try to decide if it had some merit. If I hadn't done this, I would have lost many poems while I was trying to decide whether or not to put them down on paper. This method may have produced considerable chaff — but it has also resulted in the preservation of some of my good thoughts. Most of the time I don't have any idea where a poem is going. I have to write it down in order to find out. This is also the way in which I usually wrote sermons.

Because it was my desire to make clear the infinite variety and inexhaustibility of Jesus, I have used a variety of poetic forms in this collection. Many of the poems rhyme, although this is not immediately obvious. And even the numerous free-verse poems have definite rhythms. You will find that in these I have tended to use a variation on iambic pentameter. In this way I have tried to avoid what one of my friends calls the "chopped up prose" that appears in some free-verse poetry.

Joseph Fort Newton, one of the great preachers of his time, wrote an insightful prologue to a volume entitled *Quotable Poems,* published in 1928. In it he spoke of "some of the ways in which the poet may help the preacher" — by "summing up . . . vision in a surging robe, by bringing . . . faith to a glow point of beauty."

"The lines of a poet," Newton went on to say, "if rightly used in a sermon, have a double ministry of illustration and illumination; and in the great poets often, even in lesser singers, there are lines which belong among the 'words of eternal life.' How often the poet turns on a light in an unlit room in the house of faith, or sets a candle beside a dark text of the Bible! Some of their lines open vistas half on earth and half in heaven."

Newton spoke of himself as being more in-debted to the poets than to the theologians. But he pointed out that "the poet must not preach, else his art will suffer. Nor must the preacher be purely a poet, lest he fail of his aim. Yet each may serve the other, if each keeps to his own calling and craft."

I recognize that the poet must not preach, but it is entirely possible that at times the preacher may wear the garb of the poet. And that is what I hope I have done, to some degree, in these poems.

Thomas John Carlisle
March 19, 1992

RUSH RIGHT OFF
A Modern Spiritual

Thomas John Carlisle   Thomas John Carlisle

Rush right off to get a   seat, God's ban-quet board a- waits your haste.

Be-hold, your Sov'-reign's there to greet, There's not a mo-ment left to   waste.

Chorus

So rush right off. The time's a-wast-ing. Drop ev'- ry-thing. Come on the run.

Yes, rush right off. It's time for hast-ing. Come dine with Christ, God's Cho-sen One.

XX

2 Rush right off.
Don't stop to purchase
a house or field
or any things.
Nothing on earth
is so important
as God's own feast
and joy it brings.   CHORUS

3 So rush right off.
Don't make excuse.
You sure can wait
to buy a car.
Remember this:
God's realm comes first.
How you respond
shows who you are.   CHORUS

4 So rush right off.
Even a wedding
takes second place
to this great spread.
Be dressed and on
your way rejoicing.
By God's own hand
you will be fed.   CHORUS

5 So much there is
that can distract us.
We think our petty
plans come first.
But there is only
One sufficient
to quench our hunger
and our thirst.   CHORUS

APPRECIATION

William Randolph Sengel, Marian Sengel, Sister Annunciata, Leonard J. Meinhold, Christine Burkhard Olley, Joan Donovan, George Donovan, Carol Cortelyou Cruikshank, Scott Barton, Lynda Clements, James Dowd, Margaret Shaffer Dowd, Jeanne Stevenson-Moessner, Linda Roberts-Baca, Janet DiStefano, Susan Bell, and Phyllis Trible are among a host of friends who have contributed in various ways to this manuscript.

From our own family, Thomas Dwight Carlisle, Christopher Davis Carlisle, David Livingstone Harold Carlisle, Jonathan Tristram Carlisle, Kimberly Carlisle Moore, Naomi Ruth Carlisle, and Elizabeth Carlisle Lewis have each been of special help.

Only one or two of the poems included here are among those I have written since the death of my wife, Dorothy, on January 21, 1991; this means that she shared in almost all of the poems in this collection.

Mary Hietbrink has been my editor for the fourth time. I cannot thank her enough for her continuing aid and encouragement.

Many sources have proved invaluable to me, including *Cotton Patch Parables of Liberation* by Clarence Jordan and Bill Lane Doulos and the four-volume *Gospel in Solentiname* by Ernesto Cardenal. The Congregational Library of Boston has also been an invaluable resource.

LOOKING FOR JESUS

Looking for Jesus

Looking for Jesus
I listen
to others who are searching
similarly —
wise men and women
pondering stars,
the world's workers
seeking liberation —
all who have heard
some word of life
about him or from him.
Such a company
striving together
and separately
to know what the facts are
and to interpret
accurately
and heartily
and personally.
Afraid
that what he asks
may be too much
and yet afraid
to forfeit
the Holy Grail
of his horizons.

So Many Pseudonyms

So many pseudonyms
which hide the portrait
of Jesus —
improper names
which lead our hearts
astray.

And yet a host of others
which give some clue
some component
some circumstantial evidence
some intimation
of his identity.

We cannot hope —
we should not try —
to pin him down
to pigeonhole
to make him less
than the large "more"
which must elude us.

And yet
we must not forsake
the quest
the challenge
of the profile
of his portentous
personality
ineffable
and yet intrinsic
to our journey.

I Call Him Poet

I call him poet,
healer, teacher,
savior, friend.
My list is long
and promises
to grow much longer.

Some called him imposter,
criminal, devil —
and so he was
from their perspective
which may not be
much different from mine
when I deny
the impact
of his innovations.

They knew he was a danger
to their status
and status quo
and way of living.
Sometimes I assume
there is no peril
if I probe
to know not only
who he was
but who he is
to me today.

The Gospel truth
is jeopardous
not only in each line
but in between
the lines.

Romance and Rainbow and Reality

Jesus must have chosen
not to inscribe
his story and his stories
upon papyrus
or even to edit
the product of their memories
but to allow
the centuries to guess
and wonder at
his words
his thoughts
his actions
and his claims
the culmination
and resurgence
of his life
the iridescent
romance and rainbow and reality
the memory of the music
and choreography
as they remembered him
as best they could.

6

I Look, I Listen, and I Find

So I
as best I can
reflect upon their record
the intimacy
and the enigma
of his presence
their daily joy
and their enthusiasm
their doubts and fears
and their profound immersion
in the mystery
of his re-defining
of the Messiah
who had come
to make his home with them
to share their life
in the full family
and realm of God.

No treatise
no compendium
no capsule
can capture
the superfine-ity
of Jesus.
But still I look
I listen
and I find
not only footprints
but the verity
of his amazing hereness

his approachability —
even in my denial
and betrayal —
his comradeship
his presence
and his love.

Dedicated

Like the indomitable poet
in Tennessee's *Iguana**
I hope to sing
till nearly midnight,
knowing there is no possibility
of phrasing it perfectly,
but nonetheless
baptized and wedded
and interred to words,
cradled and nurtured
by the primordial Word,
Source and Illuminator
of the verb *to be*.

*The reference is to Tennessee Williams's play entitled *The
Night of the Iguana.*

The Living Word

I have rejoiced in words
their nuances
their honey and their tart
their sounds which bless my silence
and such utterance
as stirs my heart.

Without them I am crippled
deaf and blind
and all my hope is blurred
even as I find
no life   no joy   no love
without the living Word.

John 1

Alongside Us

God dwells
in a little tent —
or hut —
alongside us.

Perhaps we might
prefer God wouldn't
clutter up our nice neighborhood
with such substandard housing!

Matthew 17:4
Mark 9:5
John 1:14
(Luke 9:33)

Doxology

How do we begin
the story of Jesus
in our Gospel?

With genealogy?
with John the Baptist?
with the basic Word?

Or with another attempt
to share the word
we have received

to tell how mothers
and babies revolutionized
our vision

to hear the song
of fathers' faith
and faithfulness

and angels'
lyric proclamation
of the great good news

beyond our understanding
and yet not beyond
our affirmation in doxology.

Luke 1 and 2
Matthew 1
Mark 1
John 1

Elizabeth and Zacharias

An old woman
now unbarren
knew the news
as soon
as Mary.

Elizabeth's child
responded
in the womb
to the blest
magnitude
of his own mission.

And his own father
lost his voice
until
he wrote
the newborn name
as John.

Luke 1:5-25, 39-45, 57-80

Only One

There is only one Jesus
but we are given four
partial — and not impartial —
portraits and we ponder
in wonder if anyone
could catch all the nuances
of such a startling man.

Jewels in His Genealogy

Tamar, Rahab, Ruth, Bathsheba —
what do these women have
in common with Jesus?

They all are mothers
of a noble line
which stretches back
in time with saving power.
Symbols of sex they seem
to uninquiring minds
who choose to miss
their genius and their passion

their penchant for survival
not primarily
for glory or celebrity
but for the sake of
lineage and heritage

their sensitivity
to rumors of God
waiting appropriation

and an extraordinary
figuration of faithfulness
over and above
their utmost dreams.

Each like Mary
magnified the Lord
in her own unexpected
and expectant way.
They shine like jewels
in his genealogy.

Matthew 1:3, 5, 6b
Luke 1:46-56
Galatians 4:4
Hebrews 11:31
James 2:25

Saturday's Song

When Holy Saturday falls on the Annunciation,
how shall we keep the Feast?
Yet both anticipate our heart's elation —
fruitful fulfillment at the very least.
Who shall prevent us as we call God's promises
to mind of Jesus made to Mary long
before when she recorded her abundant *Yes!*
This too secures Saturday's song.

Luke 1:26-38

HAS BETHLEHEM
HAPPENED TO ME?

Has Bethlehem Happened to Me?

The question which Christmas most surely
    should bring —
along with the beautiful carols we sing
and the happy excitement of trimming the tree —
is simply: Has Bethlehem happened to me?

The crèche on the mantel has everyone there —
Mary, Joseph, the shepherds, positioned with care,
and the Christ in the center for all folk to see.
But still I must ask: Is a place there for me?

For it cannot be Christmas until I stoop down
and enter a door in a faraway town
and open my heart to the farthest degree
of love: then Bethlehem will happen to me.

Luke 2:1-20

In Poetry

We speak in poetry
at Christmas
because the manger news
incites a song
which celebrates
the God who smiles upon us
in the christened child
whose face illuminates
all mornings
and all midnights.

Luke 2:13-14

17

Nativity

I did not see
the snow start.
It was all about me
before I bothered
to look out
my insulated
window.
Quieter than I
and willing
to work in small
crystallizations
it set me
thinking of One
who comes
in minimal
but basic
terms.

The Bright Glory

So sad, so shameful, when those strangers came
seeking shelter from the bitter cold
and a cradle for a child. They had no claim —
Joseph! Mary! Those names were common. They
    had no gold,
no influence to command a better place.
Only the stable offered them welcoming.
Yet that stable, lighted by love and grace,
became a palace of glory to house the King.

Luke 2:7

A Time for Kneeling

Wise men whose wisdom
might have turned to pride,
whose wealth of learning
might have given the feeling
others should bow to them,
were satisfied
to find that Christmas
is a time for kneeling.

Matthew 2:10-11

Noel

No quiet child
whose cradle gently sways
promising peaceful dreams
for all who love him.
He rocks the stable
with magnificats.
He scatters the proud.
He helps the lowly rise.
His sword cuts through
the adamants of deceit.
His cry unsettles
the victimizers
and the crucifiers
and all the extortionate
predators of his kin.
And Herod will not be
the only one to try
to stop his mouth.

Matthew 2
Luke 1, 2
Luke 23:7-12

As I Come to the Manger

Now as I come to the manger
and stand by the father and mother,
I am not here as a stranger:
I have come to see my Brother.

And though he may seem to be younger,
all history proves him the elder:
the Bread of the soul's deep hunger,
Shepherd and Savior and Shelter.

The Firstborn of many kindred,
Son of the God in whose plan
is a family of sisters and brothers:
God's aim since the world began.

Part of the Christmas promise,
part of the Christmas song,
part of the Christmas purpose
that reaches through ages long.

So now as I come to the manger
and stand by the father and mother,
I am not here as a stranger:
I have come to see my Brother.

Luke 2:16

Through Stained Glass Darkly

The lights in the window signal some concern
for prayer or faith or something less remote.
If they were candles they might resurrect
a Christmas legend tender and devout.

When they go out their dousers will go too
looking for good deeds to be done — for them.
It may be dark as Bethlehem once was.
A church is a good place to leave him.

But he is not so easy to evade
being more impertinent than we avow.
We laid him in a manger but he rose
and follows us now — and follows us now.

Christmas Basket

A Christmas basket
God brought that night
and gently laid
on our poor doorstep.
He rang the bell
but did not run away.

Christmas Pageant

We try directing
the Christmas pageant
but the script is calling
for us to be onstage
for us to listen
for us to go with haste
for us to open the inn
for us to share the stable
for us to glimpse the star.

All the parts
have not been taken yet.

Midnight Shift

There were these people, see,
working in a factory
on the night shift
late in December.
During their coffee break
one of them strolled outside
to see the stars
and then came running back
and interrupted
the indifferent conversation.
"You wouldn't believe it," she said,
"but someone in a camper
just had a child.
There's a lot of excitement,
and the ambulance is coming.
If you want to see the baby,
you'll have to hurry.
They'll be taking him
and his mother
to the Bethlehem hospital."
Several of them rushed out with her.
The others went on talking
and one of them said,
"Nothing interesting
ever happens
around here."

Good News

Simeon reminds us —
and also Anna —
that the elderly
need not give up
despite infirmities
and weaknesses
which age bestows.

The warmth of faith,
the mind's intense desire
can burgeon, bless,
and grow to glory.

Luke 2:22-38

There Came Wise Men

Who is it now desiring words with me
about a child who wants to be a king?
Speak to them gently. Do not let them see
your spears behind their backs. The gifts they bring
are for another. Say I do not care.
But why has none of all my agents filed
the name or town of this conspirator?
Most diligently let them seek the child.
Enroll them all as my unwitting spies.
They will be none the wiser. At their word,
wherever in Judea this lamb lies,
my gift to him will be an assassin's sword.

Matthew 2:1-12, 16-18

Getting Lost

"Mary and Joseph also took Jesus to the temple . . .
when he got lost on them."
— Alejandro in *The Gospel in Solentiname*
by Ernesto Cardenal

The peasant's words
provoked my pondering
when he described the incident
in the great temple
when Jesus *got lost on them*

and made me wonder
how often Jesus
gets lost on me
and I become the one
who's really lost.

Luke 2:41-50

Hangup

My, how you've changed, Jesus,
since we first met you
in Sunday school. You've grown
and we haven't. That seems
to be our hangup.

Luke 2:52

HIS REAL HUMANITY

His Real Humanity

Did he get hot
when the temperature
shot up
or tired
when the road
was arduous
or dirty
with dust
fatigued by work
depleted
when he opened
the floodgates
of his love
or offered
a transfusion
from his veins?

If not
why not?

John 4:6

The Shadow Side

The shadow side of Jesus
is a way of saying
he wrestled with the risks
his strengths exacted

the miraculous means
which served no higher ends

the daredevil leap
to titillate the crowd

the mountain view
of worlds to rule and ruin

and he discovered
how to deal
with all the demons
which embraced his world.

Matthew 4:1-11, 16:23
Mark 1:12-13, 8:33
Luke 4:1-13

And All Her Memories

Was it important
for Jesus
to turn water
into wine?

He thought so.

Not principally because
his mother asked him
so peremptorily.
Rather because
he recognized
how much it meant
to a young girl's
happiness
and all her memories.

John 2:1-11

Disability

I am not so good
at making people happy
at wedding feasts.
I can't provide
the sparkle that turns
water into wine.

John 2:1-11

Not All

Not all the Pharisees
not all the publicans
not all the prostitutes
merited the pejorative* label.

Jesus knew
that Nicodemus
as one of the
meliorative examples
was able
like the best —
and worst — of us
to go a further mile
to know another birth
and share and spread the love
of God's domain on earth.

John 3:1-21

*Since *pejorative* implies a negative meaning, *meliorative*
  could be the opposite.

Mutual Ministry

Jesus found
a number
of wealthy
philanthropists

(in the true
derivation
of that word) —
lovers of humankind
like Nicodemus
Joseph of Arimathea
and even lately
Zacchaeus
as well as all the women
who contributed
to his uncommon cause.

They had the knack
of knowing how to
negotiate the needle's eye
of generosity
concern and caring
that gave them access
to the Realm of God.

So hard
and yet
so easy
with Jesus lending
the special thread.

Matthew 19:24
Mark 10:25
Luke 18:25

Jesus to Nicodemus

"Come in," he said,
at Nicodemus' knock.
"You need not be afraid —
at least of me.
Even if someone sees you,
as a teacher
you have a right
to explore by day or night
the fountain of truth.
Perhaps you know too much
of law and custom,
scrolls of scholarship
and erudition
which in its finicky
fastidious way
may close your eyes
and ears and heart
to the priorities
of God. I hope
you come again to tell
your own experience
of death and birth.
Eternal life
is waiting at your door."

John 3:1-21

One of Many Ways

How sad when we insist
on limiting
our spiritual vocabulary
or on making
a cliché
of life's best
and most incredible
experience.

Being "born again"
is one of many ways
of trying to describe
the joy and grace
when one becomes
truly a new creature
in Christ Jesus.

John 3:3-9

Christmas in Samaria

WHAT!
What are you thinking of,
what are you trying to do —
a Jew, a rabbi,
asking to share a drink
from the same water jar
with me,
proscribed as both
Samaritan and woman
beside this well of Sychar
where Jacob drank his full
in time now immemorial?

You talk with me
as though I were no stranger,
as though I were a learnéd *man*
of noble character
and able to imbibe
your teachings.

Get out of here!
No — I don't really mean *that*.
You even deign to talk
theology with me.
No longer which mountain is better
in our land or Jerusalem.
The only perfect place,
you say, is everywhere
we worship God
in spirit and in truth.

I am confused
and at the same time captivated
by all you tell me
regarding the living water
you can provide
to quench my thirsty soul
and rescue me
from my poor parched existence,
I who have failed
to hold my former husbands
to their vows
and am helpless now
to engage my current friend
in legal marriage.
How did you guess —
or know —
my tragedy?
How do you
understand me
like you do?

Wait here
and let me shout it to the town
that Christ has come.

John 4:3-43

Well-Alibied

Jews and Samaritans
did not drink
out of the same vessels
or use the same
drinking fountains
or the same liturgy —
which makes us
feel either
superior
or sympathetic
because of our own
well-alibied
exclusions.

John 4

As in Nazareth

It sounded beautiful
at first
just as it does to us.
Like his hometown audience
we too have second
thoughts as to the viability
of the demands
of such a savior.
Where do *we* go
when we parade
out from our pews?
To the village cliff
with violent expression
of our repudiation?
Or to the marketplace
with promise of participation?

Luke 4:16-30

Zinger

To the pure all things are pure.
How true and apropos
until we look within and ask:
But how are we to know?

Matthew 5:8
Titus 1:15
(and a phrase from
George A. Buttrick)

Welcome?

Is Jesus
welcome
on this turf —
my city
my campus
or my church?

Or is he able
to do no mighty work
in my locality
because of my
hostility or my
inhospitality?

Matthew 13:58
Luke 4:16-30

In Love's Defense

How beautiful
in love's defense
the virtue of
faithfulness in
nonviolence.

Matthew 5:39
Luke 6:29
Matthew 26:52

No Joke

The threats of Christ
are buried
in the brutal Bible.

Woe to you all
who now are rich
for you have had
your joy.

And woe to you
who find so many
cruel ingenious ways
of playing hypocrite.

Depart from me, you cursed,
who see me in the stranger,
the hungry, thirsty, naked, sick,
and do not do
one blessed thing
for these who bear
my image and my love.

The threats of Christ
are buried
in the brutal Bible
and we are fools
to think that he
was only fooling.

Matthew 23:13-26; 25:41-46
Luke 6:24

Preservative

Salt of the earth
we're called to be
but if we're not
the world will rot.

Matthew 5:13

CHRIST, YOU CARRIED A FLOWER

Christ, You Carried a Flower

Christ, you carried
a flower in your hand
more often than not.
Your beard
reddened and curled
beside the exuberant
shore. You walked barefoot
at times. You laid
the airless mattress of your robe
under the pitch of stars.
Your knapsack held
original water
elemental bread.
You practiced
the discipline of love
and faith's abandon.

Matthew 4:18
Mark 10:32
John 21:4

Christ the Tiger

They call him
Christ the Tiger
when they hear
the shocking things
he said about plucked-out eyes
and other members
which offend against
our eligibility
to qualify for God's
society in earth and heaven.

Translate the metaphors
as freely as we will
we cannot turn
his terms to mush
or make believe
he asks no discipline
or sacrifice
within the terrible
and terrifying
lines he lays
for our approval
and our ultimate
allegiance.

Matthew 5:29-30; 18:6-9
Mark 9:42-50

Hymn of the Penitent Pharisees

We are the Pharisees who sing
our songs to Jesus who decried
treating the spirit as a thing
to be evaded and denied.

Our pride is in a Savior who
would blast our wan conformities.
He died for championing the new
and dangerous. We worship ease.

We ring the changes on his death
to circumvent his victory,
reiterate some shibboleth
and think we mean "Abide with me."

Oh teach us, Prophet of the love
that will not let your people go,
till we become enamored of
the faith you came that we might know.

Help us admit what hypocrites
we still inevitably are
and grant us still your benefits
although we follow from afar.

> Matthew 6:2, 5, 16; 7:5
> Luke 6:42; 13:15
> (and numerous other passages)

Interchange

Once in a while
we take God seriously
and find what fun
the enterprise can be.

Matthew 6:33

Letters to God

I am always
writing illeg
ible letters
to God asking
asking for this
for that and I
leave them around
unsigned unstamped
and with no self
addressed enve
lope for reply
and to my a
mazement I get
answers answers
I cannot be
lieve but I do
and I go on
writing letters
to God to God

Matthew 7:7-11

Our Blasphemy

Must we be
just polite
to Jesus?
That's another
neat way
to get him
out of the way
sidetrack him
minimize
his mandate.
Be polite.
Yes sir.
Be polite
but keep him
from being Lord
to us.

Luke 6:46

Women Only

Only prophets
priests and elders
felt empowered
to anoint
the earliest kings
of Judah and Israel,
pouring the ointment
on the royaled heads
of Saul and David and Solomon.

Samuel, Zadok, Nathan
certified who they believed
to be God's choice
in ritual we perceive
as unfamiliar
and even bizarre.

When we come to Jesus,
the disguised
unrecognized
and unidentified
child of the Sovereign
of the Universe,
we discover women —
only women
women only —
have the insight
to accept the honor
of anointing him
the already and future king
of all the world.

And so they pour
the ointment
and they lavish
their homage and devotion
in a way
we only dimly
try to understand.

1 Samuel 10:1; 16:13
2 Samuel 5:3
1 Kings 1:34, 39, 45
Mark 14:3-9
Luke 7:36-50
John 12:3-8

The House Where Jesus Lived

I had never noticed
the house where Jesus lived.
The Gospels mention it
so unobtrusively
and do not say
whose house it was
or just how long he lived there
or whether it was his headquarters
even on farther journeys
as well as when
he walked to work
each morning.

He taught beside the lake,
in the mountains,
along the highways,
in synagogues when welcome,
and at times
crowds thronged the house
where Jesus lived.

Would I have dared —
or cared —
to knock upon his door?

Matthew 13:1, 36; 17:25
Mark 2:1; 7:17; 9:33; 10:10

Double Lock

Faith and forgiveness
are the secret keys
releasing us
from our paralysis.

Luke 5:20

We Are the Sequel

Exasperating
to know so little
of the early Christians

to wonder where
the rest of the disciples
traveled and what they did

to learn no more
of Mary Magdalene,
the "other" Mary
and Joanne

or whether
the Rich Young Ruler
or the Woman at the Well
or the Canaanitish Mother
or the Lad with Loaves and Fishes
have sequels to their stories.

Lucky indeed
that we possess as much
as the authentic
narrative divulges,
and hints enough
of Jesus' way
of caring
and communicating,
to give rich guidelines
for all subsequent
and presentday disciples
who hear the call
the earliest heard
and make their personal
and jubilant commitment.

Something about Jesus

They trusted Jesus —
all these men and women.
They wanted to get well
and they believed
he wished them well
and had the will and power
to make them whole.
While some had let them down
others had opened doors —
and roofs — and journeyed miles
to make his healing touch —
or word — available.

There must have been
something about Jesus
that destroyed their doubts
and fired their faith.

Mark 2:1-12
John 5:7-13

Investing in Jesus

Would you have invested in Jesus,
gambled whatever money you had,
borrowed on your real and personal
property as the months went by
so that this traveling company
could keep equipped and fed for the journey?

Some people did —
a Mary or more, Joanne, Susanna.
The list was not entered
in full at the security exchange
and what they contributed
did not count as a tax deduction.
But they gave and kept on giving
never expecting any return
but what they had already received
a thousand times over.

Would you invest in Jesus?

Luke 8:2-3

Gainful Employment

I often wonder
if there might have been
room for one more
in the gallant and joyful group
of friends and followers —
the men and women
who left their jobs
their nets and offices
their dust- and dish-pans
to be with Jesus
and to try to do
the big and little things
which he requested
or suggested
or inspired.
He was the kind of person
able to find a place
for the least likely
and even the come-lately.

Would *I* have said,
"I'm otherwise —
and much more profitably —
employed"?

For Me?

The stories Jesus told
never grow old.
Their afterlife
goes on and on.
His extrasensitive
perception penetrates
the hardness of
our ultramodern hearts
until we ask,
Could he
have meant these words
for me?

O Christ,
you are our poet and musician
and so much more.

Waiting for Harvest Time

Jesus told another story of good seed —
in a fruitful field this time
but while the sower slept
his enemy arrived
armed with seeds of weeds
and scattered them discriminately
throughout the plot.
And when the field was filled
with this menacing mixture
the sower did not dare
attempt to extract
the troublesome tares
but had to wait
till harvest time
when they might be segregated —
the weeds to the bonfire
and the wheat
to the granary.

If we have ears
we may hear Jesus saying
how hatred hurts
how love makes fruitful
and how intertwined they are
in us and others.

Matthew 13:24-30, 36-43

Another Seed

Another seed
attracted the attention
of the timeless teacher

one so very small —
the mustard seed
that grows to such a height
the birds have ample room
to make their nests
among the branches.

So love can grow
from very small beginnings
to make a heaven on earth.

Matthew 13:31-32

Rising Power

Three measures of meal —
the housewife's standard recipe —
mixed with the yeast
which seems so insignificant
but turns the dough to bread.

God's country grows
with the same rising power.

Matthew 13:33
Luke 13:21

Who Will Buy?

And who will buy
the treasure-laden field,
the perfect pearl,
the new birthright of Christ?

Matthew 13:44-45

POET AND TROUBADOUR

Poet and Troubadour

Well versed he was
in celebrating life
in luminous lives
authored in the aridity
of desert spaces.
His lyric language
his magic minstrelsy
the fire of his phrases
his matchless metaphors and images
came down from the mountain
to transpose   transfix   transfigure
the idiom of our plain.

Matthew 14:13; 13:33
Mark 6:46
John 6:15

What Difference?

What difference
does it make
whether he walked
on water
if he makes it
to me
through all the waves
my world is making!

Matthew 14:22-27
John 6:16-21

Mistaken Identity

The success story
of Jesus
leaves some elements
of embarrassment
to the particular
observers
of his original
acts and intentions.

He made waves
then how is it
he's such a calmer
in some circles now
and rocks no boats?

Who do we take him for?

Without cross-purposes?

Ego Sum: "It is I"

Do we dare
ask Who he is?
He comes.
His coming is a sign
but still we ask
for other signs
and disregard the sign

his coming states.
He comes.
Sometimes we recognize him
look him in the face
observe his hands
and say "My Lord!"

More often fear
or blindness
hides his wholeness
and his holiness
and we avert
our eyes and estimation.

In the storm
and night
he walks across
the waters of our world
baptized by waves
and lit by lightning
till we cry "A ghost!"
He is no more a ghost
than you or I
but still we cry
"What do we have
to do with you
or you with us,
you wraith of hope
and righteousness?"
For terror
is our trademark
and our burial cave.

He comes.
Makes it to us
poor rowers that we are
makes it to us
and satisfies our questions
before we lip the words.
He comes and says
"Yes, it is I.
Take heart and hope."

Matthew 14:27-28
Mark 6:50
Luke 24
John 6:20-21

Nourished

Five thousand plus
our Jesus fed
and still we are
not surfeited
when with the mass
of folk he feeds
we too are nourished
in our needs.

Matthew 14:13-21
Mark 6:30-44
Luke 9:10-17
John 6

Breakaway

Since Jesus was conditioned
by his culture
he had to break away
and face the consequences —
for treating foreigners
and children
and women
with respect.

No Wonder She Won

Men were adroit
though not successful
in one-upping him.
When this woman talked back
Jesus admired
her spunk
her humor
and her total
commitment
to having
her daughter healed.
No wonder
she won.

Matthew 15:21-28
Mark 7:24-30

Stranger from Syria

Delicious repartee
in what she said.
A matter of life and health
and faith that penetrated
beyond all borders.

Matthew 15:21-28
Mark 7:24-30

Help the Blind

Heal me, O Jesus,
as you healed the blind:
Bethsaida's blind man,
Jericho's Bartimeus.

Help me see gradually
if you desire
or in an instant of insight
if you choose.

But miracle my seeing
so I may
divine your grace
and join you in your journey.

Mark 8:22-26; 10:46
Luke 18:35-43

Heal Me

Heal me, I pray,
of all that bars and blinds me
from perceiving your presence
and your patient providence.

Mark 8:22-26; 10:46

More than Metaphor

Jesus' striking statement
calling for carrying crosses
was challenging
and impressive
and implausible
hyperbole
until he took himself
literally.

Matthew 10:38; 16:24
Mark 8:34; 10:21
Luke 9:23; 14:27

But Living It

We love to quote
what Jesus said
but living it
might strike us dead.

Matthew 16:24-25

Transfiguration

Encompassed
by the mystery
of God
they saw
and did not see
listened
and hardly heard
yet it transfigured them
as well as him.

Matthew 17:1-8
Mark 9:2-8
Luke 9:28-36

Downs and Ups

I wish that Jesus
had not said so clearly
those on the top drop down
and those on the bottom rise.
As long as I
retain my smug pretensions
I'm in for one
spectacular surprise.

Matthew 19:30
Mark 10:31
Luke 13:30

No Heart

They had no heart
to attack the woman
once Jesus forced them
to cross-examine
themselves as well as her.

No heart —
which was their problem
in the first place.

John 8:3-11

Unapplied

I shudder
at each stone
they might have thrown
but do not want to see
how it applies to me.

John 8:3-11

All Stones

Jesus left
all stones unturned
as far as throwing them
at others was concerned.

John 8:3-11

71

No Stone

No stone
in Jesus'
rugged hand.
Instead he wrote
imperishably
in the sand.

John 8:3-11

Chivalry

The chivalry of Jesus
is exposed:
he does not stare
at the beleaguered woman
as some are wont to do
but stoops and writes
in the uncensorious sand
before he rises
with the gaze of love.

John 8:3-11

Light of the World

I call him Light —
Light of the World —
and yet prefer
to try to hide
in darkness.

John 8:12-18
John 9:5

Invitation to Truth

We live on bread and water
when we might
exchange our prison fare
for food and freedom
and eternal light.

John 8:32

Our Language

Jesus spoke
the language
of his listeners,
articulating
their everyday
experiences,
joys, problems,
opportunities —
the dark side
of brightness
and the bright side
of darkness —
and expects us
to translate
his stories
to our time,
our language,
our locality.

Where Did Jesus Live?

Where did Jesus live?
Inconsequential question?
Of course at home in Nazareth
for all those growing years.
But in the fruitful
fateful final years, what then?

Foxes have holes, he said,
and birds have nests
but as for him he owned
no permanent address.
He took no thought of home.
Always available
a friendly roof of stars
all air-conditioned.

How about a wayside inn
where a certain Samaritan
asked the innkeeper
for convalescent
quarters for the mugged man
he found along the road?

Would *you* have urged
that he stop any time
and share your bed and breakfast
providing this
did not require hosting
all the disciples too?

I do not have the answer.
But do you?

Matthew 8:20; 6:34
Luke 10:29-37

Almost Midnight

My neighbor
(half a world away)
pounds on my door
and yells
for food
and it is almost midnight
for us both.

Luke 11:5-10

LIBERATION STORY

Liberation Story

I am a woman older than my age,
bent and deformed by my paralysis
these eighteen years,
my inability to look
another straight in the eyes
my hardest cross.

Now how could Jesus care
to notice me or dare to call me over
to the more sacred, privileged place
allowed to men in any synagogue,
and on the Sabbath day — the Sabbath day! —
to heal me with a simple word of freedom
sealed with a touch — a touch! —
which might have made him
unclean for all he knew?

They tried to blame me —
though it was worth the charge to be thus freed.
Their anger was at him for all the rules
he cavalierly broke on my behalf —
and on behalf of everyone who sees
the meaning of the way he treated me.

I praise my God and his for what he did
in lifting up my body and my soul.
And I shall tell my liberation story —
your liberation story —
our liberation story —
always,
always.

Luke 13:10-17

Call to Freedom

How can I change
when I have chosen to put
my eggs in different
baskets to protect
all my positions
and to cover
all the bases
of my little diamond?

The crisis
which Jesus Christ
brings to my judgment
is not resolved
by gradual osmosis
but by my metamorphosis
to the demands
of his extraordinary freedom.

Luke 13:24

Other Fish to Fry

We don't hate Jesus.
We adore his name
and say it sometimes
sanctimoniously
but keep him in his place
with great success
because we are
so busy being loyal
to our own land

(the one we love)
and business
(one has to live!)
and home and friends
(God bless them all)
there isn't time
or opportunity
to take his words to heart
or talk and walk with him.

Matthew 10:37; 13:1-9

Mark 4:1-9

Luke 8:4-8; 14:16-33

And Still Today

Deep healing —
the dynamics
of Jesus' journey
through a wounded world.

God's Banquet

You think
if you don't come
nobody will.
So you exert
your option
for refusal —
too busy
for the banquet
God is throwing.

Come now:
You aren't
all that important.
The realm of God
arrives with
or without you.

Rejoice that you
were lucky enough
to get an invitation
and rush right off
to take the lowest seat.

Luke 14:15-24
Luke 14:7-11

Family Portrait

Jesus is great at painting pictures:
the feast where the whole family
of God is present — with the exception
of those who choose the hell of being absent.

Luke 14:16-24

Lost Judgment

We lose the parables
about the *lost* —
lost sheep
lost coin
lost sons —
unless we find
why we consider
God's concern unfair.

Luke 15

Family Affair

This brother of yours —
God says —
this sister of yours
(who happen to be
my son, my daughter)
I love
as much as I love you.
No less, no more
just prodigally.

Luke 15:32

Too Late

Too rich to give
a moment's thought
to the sorry beggar
daily at his gate,
he waited
to repent
his callous crime
until too late

too late

too late.

Luke 16:19-31

The Measure

The things that don't disturb us are the measure
of who and what we are.
To care would cost too much of what we treasure.
We settle in as far
from God's design as we can travel
and give ourselves discreetly to the devil.

Luke 16:19-31

Signal for Celebration

The music starts —
the pipe and drum —
the song and dance
of feast and celebration.

Can we be eager
to join the joy
even when we
are not the guest of honor?

Luke 15:24-32

Reconciliation

The father
does not follow
our feeble example
with judgment
criticism
raw rejection
but from a wounded heart
still tenders love.

Luke 15:24-32

The Death of God

Give me my full inheritance, he said,
as if his father were already dead.

I want mine too while it is still available —
the older son with logic unassailable.

And they — and we — want God out of the way.
"Give me" becomes our favorite phrase to pray.

Luke 15:11-32

Role Model

This woman —
persistent, aggressive, determined —
is an apt role model
for all those
who hunger for justice
in today's society.

The unjust judges,
the sharks,
the exploiters,
the vultures,
the victimizers —
all get their comeuppance
when they come up against
a stance like hers.

Luke 18:2-5

Wide Receivers

We who are
the wide receivers
of so much
of God's abundant mercy
may presume
we merit
even more.

Luke 17:5-10

Monologue

My most conspicuous gift
is arrogance
although I call it
by a nicer name.
Deserving of God's grace,
I take each chance
to re-remind God
of my moral fame.

No groveling for me.
I can recite
my virtues every time
I happen to pray.
I'm sure I'm God's
particular delight.
I wish that Jesus' words
would go away.

Luke 18:9-14

Right Where I Am

O Christ, I fear
the fallacy for me
is urging others
with clever, stinging words
to turn and follow you
while I remain
busily behind
right where I am.

Redemption

The sweep
of Jesus' words,
his kind
of caring,
his ruthful
honesty,
his acute
perspectives,
his courage
clearly crosswise,
astonish
and redeem
our brokenness.

Encounters

Jesus wasn't a soft touch —
or was he?
Not indifferent to sin
and how it hurt
the doer and the done to.
Neither ignoring
nor ignorant.
Critical when required.
More often gentle
sufferable
and always catching sight
of God within each one
he came across.

The Limits of Generosity

We are all-fired annoyed
when someone gets
God's generosity in equal measure
to what we gain for working longer hours.

We choose subtraction
as the equitable
and mathematical computation

but God knows how to add
although we don't.

Matthew 20:1-16

They Could Not Comprehend

Three times he told them.
Once was not enough.
And still they couldn't believe
how much he meant it.

He set his face
to make the uphill journey
Jerusalem demanded
with the certain jeopardy
that lay in God's own city.

Three times he told them
he must suffer and die.
And thrice was not enough.
They could not comprehend
that kind of ending
for either them or him.

Matthew 16:21-28; 17:22-23; 20:17-19
Mark 8:31–9:1; 9:30-32; 10:32-34
Luke 9:22-27, 51-53; 9:43b-45; 18:31-34
John 10:15, 17; 12:25

Unlike Zacchaeus

I too am little like Zacchaeus —
whatever my height may happen to be.
It will take more than a tall tree
to give me a glimpse of Jesus.
Whatever riches I may possess,
however fairly or unfairly gained,
if in their usage I have disdained
the service of God, they are utterly worthless.
Were I with joy to quit my perilous perch,
come down, welcome him in my home,
I too might know the marvel of the lost
who have yielded to God's search.
It will be a miracle if I come:
I am too good — too good — at counting the cost.

Luke 19:1-10

"I am the Resurrection and the Life"

Jesus could not become
the resurrection and the life
by lifting Lazarus
from his stone-sealed tomb.

The Bethany grave
was a Gethsemane
which prayed the way
for Jesus' own
incarceration
and release.

No wonder he is troubled —
deeply moved — and weeps.

The gravecloth
is the sign
of his undoing
the damages of death
and speaking still and now
the triumphant words.

John 11:11-54

AGENTS PROVOCATEURS

Agents Provocateurs

Always trying
to arrest Jesus
they plotted questions
which could get him
into trouble.
He pleaded
no fifth amendment
but with a wry
and ready wit
recast their arguments
and undermined
their moot maneuvers
their deft intrigues
and left them handcuffed
to their premises.

Caiaphas and Company

Caiaphas and Company
complained:
        That crowd
shouldn't desecrate
our holy city
with their decibels
of hurrahs
and hosannas
and their literal
harvest of palms
and waveables.

Quiet please
for the benefit
of those who have retired
from the generous agenda
compatible with peace.

Matthew 21:1-11
Mark 11:1-10
Luke 19:28-40
John 12:12-15

Triumphal Entry

Into a world
of misfits
losers
crooks
and chiselers
harlots
hypocrites
Herods
and even
people like me
Jesus came
and made a drastic
difference.

Shatterer

Jesus, you clang
and clash
the cymbals
shattering
our quaint complacence
just as you did
that first Palm Sunday
when the wild parade
was unpoliceable,
just as that day
you stormed the Temple
and took the crooked
moneychangers and the sheepish
salesmen by surprise.
If we are wise
we welcome
your guerrilla raids
upon *our* somnolent
self-satisfaction.

Matthew 21:12-17
Mark 11:15-19
Luke 19:45-48
John 2:13-18; 12:12-19

No Tickertape or Porsche

Not tickertape
or pussy willows
but palms
engaged the celebration
as the hosanna
procession shouted
and shouldered its way
into the Holy City.

And not a Porsche
plush with the latest options
or even a pickup truck
but the very cheapest vehicle
the nation knew
illustrating the absence
of pride and pomp
and blood and thunder
which were scorned
by this strange sovereign
with the passionate heart
now set to suffer
and complete his mission.

Matthew 21:1-11
Mark 11:1-10
Luke 19:28-40
John 12:12-15

Holy Fury

Ugly behavior
on the part of Jesus
as he raided
the House of God
where mercenary men
usurped its function.

We act askew
when Jesus' passion —
his thirst and hunger —
for simple justice
does not exact
the fury of our faith.

Matthew 5:6; 21:12-17
Mark 11:15-19
Luke 19:45-48
John 2:13-17

Betrayer

Who was the betrayer?

One who said
"I come with you"
and went the other way.

Matthew 21:28-32

Tenant

God's vineyard
I have treated
as my own.

I have not shared
the harvest
with God's children.

I tell God's Son
to go get lost
while I

claim title
to the fruit
that is not mine.

Matthew 21:33-46
Mark 12:1-12
Luke 20:9-19

The Pleasure of His Company

He calls us
to be happy.
Was he ever
happy himself
or only
a man of sorrows
closeted with grief?

We ought to know
better and hear
the ring of laughter
in his party
and the celebration
for every prodigal
whom he helped home.

The pleasure
of his company
outjoys
all feasts.

Love Does Not End

Love does not end
as all else must,
does not surrender
to the storm or to the dust,
endures although endangered,
wounded yet will heal,
adamant as diamonds,
stubborn as steel.

Jesus Wept

Jesus wept
over the serenity
and stupidity
of the city
whose business
blotted out
the weightier matters
of equal law
and positive peace.

Luke 19:41

Jesus Knew

She had given
her last
and little coin.
She had no more
to give
but Jesus knew
how great the gift
how true
his own strange words:
Blessed —
yes, *blessed* —
happy
are the poor.

Matthew 5:3
Mark 12:41-44
Luke 6:20; 21:1-4

Seamless

All of a piece
the seamless
death and life
of Jesus.

His parables
his passion for the poor
his healing touch
his daily walk
analogous
to cross
and resurrection.

He makes us whole
and we must see him
wholly.

At Home

Each night
Jesus went back
to Bethany
that harrowing
and holy week —
spent an entire
day there
in the midst of it —

at home
with Lazarus
and Mary
and Martha
who partly understood
the crucial floodgate
of the trauma
of his decision,
the reckless malice
of his enemies,
the terror
of the cross
he spoke about
so seriously.
How good
to have such friends
to feel the warm
embrace of affection
and acceptance.

Would Jesus feel at home
with me? or you?

Matthew 21:17
Mark 11:11-12
Luke 21:37-38

Too Tough?

I do not like to hear
of being cast
into the outer darkness
or of melancholy
and inglorious
weeping accompanied
by gnashing teeth.

I do not like to think
of servants being slaughtered
for their faithlessness —
their disregard of duty
and of privilege.

Isn't Jesus
too tough
on our apostasy
our dereliction
and infidelity
our betrayal
of his cause?

Matthew 25:14-30
Luke 19:11-27

Ab(so)lution

Did Jesus need cleaning up?
Perish the thought, we mutter.
No bathtubs, no running water,
no advertised deodorants.

We do not know the details.

But we get a whiff of how
one woman found a way
to show what life and death —
to show what death and life —
significance he held for her
and might for all the world.

Matthew 26:6-13

Like Judas

Like Judas
I like
success
safety
et cetera.

Is my greed
as great
as his
or my ambition
as smooth
or my hypocrisy
as eloquent
or my treachery
as courteous —
the kiss
and tell
of my lackluster
lovelessness?

Is my remorse
more tardy
and less real
than his?

Matthew 10:4; 26:14
Mark 3:19; 14:10
Luke 6:16; 22:3
John 6:71; 13:2, 26

GUEST AND HOST

Guest and Host

Jesus was forever
changing places.
Guest or host
he managed both
superlatively.
He needed people
much as they needed him
and did not blush
to suffer the risk
of being rejected
in either role.

He entertained
as lord or visitor,
a generous soul
who also reaped
the largesse of his company.
He found it blesséd
to receive as well as give.
He did it all
with perfect graciousness:
the guest and host
of our humanity.

Farewell Party

We see that supper
in the borrowed room
on someone's second floor
as ornate and sedate
as a church service
with ushers at the door
dealing out bulletins
and an organist
softpedaling mood music
and a preacher passing out
small slices of gray matter
to apathetic patrons

When all the time
it was a party
a farewell party
with the guest of honor
serving as host
the only one aware
that he was leaving
on the midnight train.
They would remember
how he raised the cup
and drank to them.

Matthew 26:17-30
Mark 14:12-26
Luke 22:7-38
John 13:2–18:1

Behind Closed Doors

The cloak and dagger
elements of communion
escape us. In the hideout
on the second floor
he shattered all easy
notions of sustenance.
He reconstituted bread.
He made wine viable.
He revealed the unspeakable
four-letter password —
a new substantiation of
love.

Matthew 26:17-30
Mark 14:12-26
Luke 22:7-38
John 13:2–18:1

Embrace

The bread that Jesus
shares with me
bids me embrace
his whole family.

John 6

Remembering

Remembering
him
we take
the bread
and cup
so that we may
remember
every moment
every day.

Seascape

Around their supper table was a sea
and they were swimming conscious of its shore
able to grip the cup of mystery
and reach the bread. It was a restless floor
beneath their feet. Their host by lifted word
was keeping them from sinking through despair.
"This is my blood and flesh" was what they heard
and wondered if they dreamed that he was there
or whether they had fallen all asleep
some silent night when fish were hard to take.
But then he summoned them to leave the deep —
or did he say to drink it for his sake?
And which was caught within his own fouled net?
And who was surer than the rooster's morn?
"Master, is it I who will forget?"
and "Were it better I had not been born?"

The sea dissolved but he remained the same
known friend yet more than anyone could know
or compass with a picture or a name.
"One song," he said, "and then we have to go."

Matthew 26:20-30
Mark 14:12-26
Luke 22:7-38
John 13:2–18:1

On the Same Night

"One song," he said, "and then we have to go."
They sang it lustily before they went.
Familiar as it was, they were not sure
exactly what it meant. They did not need
to know — but someday would recall they sang.

Their going was a passing through a wall.
Each carved out for himself a jagged hole
and squirmed and squeezed to reach the fairer air
outside the city's smog and affluence.
No gate is silhouetted to the man.

Their going was a gradual descent.
Each picked his footing on the moonlit slope
and hoped the clattering stones would leave his stair
firm-set to let himself the easier down.
Each chose the pattern for his own decline.

Their going was the crossing of a brook
where one might wash his hands and one his lips
and one his eyes. Their feet were earlier clean.
His basin had washed. His towel had dried.
His word had freed them for the bonds of service.

Their going was a crisscrossed patient climb
to meet a garden marked with olive trees.
It had not looked so much like this before.
But time was moving at a stranger pace.
They moved but were not sure they moved
    with him.

Their going was his going but their steps
were not his steps. Their prayer was not his prayer.
Their eyes were not inclined to stay awake
although they dimly heard his last request.
They could not bring themselves to share his night.

Lower than theirs and higher was the way
he took. He would not make them rise and sing
the song of sorrow but he wove the notes
to turn their three-day threnody to joy
and summon alleluias to their hearts.

Matthew 26:30, 36-46
Mark 14:32-42
Luke 22:39-46
John 18:1-11

Elements for a Sacrament

It was the place of a skull
the hill of crossed wood
and of crushed bones.

It was a place of great pain
and no good day ever
until he came.

It was the sixth day of the week
when he arrived at the top
and joined the drama

with elements for a sacrament
fresh as April
and more nourishing.

The consecration
was fleshed in
by lifted hands.

When he had finished
the whole world
was invited.

Matthew 27:33-56
Mark 15:22-41
Luke 23:33-49
John 19:17-30

Shalom

I too was trying
to get comfortable
when he let me have it
with that passionate word
Peace
with its odor
of indiscriminate
love.

John 14:27; 16:33

I Have Called You Friends

I have called you friends, says Jesus,
but there are times no one would ever guess it —
friends of each other, friends of mine.
You call each other names.
You impugn each other's honor.
You covet the best assignment
and the most gratifying credit
even when you are working for yourselves.
Forgiveness and reconciliation
get lost in the turmoil of your quarrels.
Friends make the most successful enemies
when they lose touch with each other,
when they lose touch with me, says Jesus.
Nonetheless, *I have called you friends.*

John 15:15

Entitlement

Just because
I know the name
of Jesus —
and approve
of some of the more
comfortable words
his friends recorded —
hardly entitles me
to qualify
as one of his
more faithful
and deserving followers.

Hungry Like a Fox

Herod hungered
for happiness
but would have settled
for a little bit of wit
or a larger slice of kingdom.
He hankered
for the good opinion
of headstrong prophets
and promising dancers
but could not reconcile
his contradictory appetites.

Like his father
he could make fun
out of funerals.
Jests were more to his taste
than justice
while compassion
cost more than he cared to pay.
He might have enjoyed
being a hero
if he could have
sandwiched it in.

                                    Luke 23:7-12

UNDER THE SUN

Under the Sun

Under the sun
there was no one
to comfort them
sons of oppression
daughters of fears
no one to comfort them
none to explain to them
none to sedate
sores and torments
and tears.

Under the sun
there was no one
to speak for them
no one to cry for them
under the sun
save for a brother
they treated as traitor
the tender
compassionate
grief-bearing one.

Some set their faces
in anger
against him.
Some double-crossed him
and some let him down.
Under the sun
there is none
who can help us
save for the healer
with hands like our own.

Hands like our own
but all ruddy
and bloody
bent by the burdens
he wittingly chose.
Committing himself
to a cross
of crude hardwood.
Under the sun
we have one friend
God knows.

Crucifixion

They had to kill him
to stop him.
They did
and they didn't.

Matthew 27:33-56
Mark 15:22-41
Luke 23:33-49
John 19:17-30

Criminal

Jesus wasn't in jail long.
Abhorrence of his crime
demanded as instant a death
as courts and schedules
could afford. The Lord of life
had violated treasured
values and upset
the neverchangers
of temple and government.
They could not forgive him
what they knew they thought he did.

Forgive

Forgive him
if he speaks
unseemly words
prompted by pain
disappointment
abandonment.
Forgive him
if he tells off
the velvet blackguards
who thought his death
would make life easier
for them
and all the jestive
throng.

A curse
might be worth
something
at such
a juncture.
At the least:
Woe unto them.
But no.
He knows
his own
commandment
knows they do not
know their own
doing and undoing.
Lifts them up
in love
and full committal:
Father, forgive them.

                                    Luke 23:34

Even Now; Even Less

His suffering
we cannot stomach
so we devote
a minimum
of time and meditation
to the hours
he agonized
upon the cross.

Even less
do we care
to think about
the sufferings
of others
of God's children
even now
across this perilous planet.

Father, forgive us
for we do
not want to care
to know.

Luke 23:34

Remember

I must
remember
his intense concern
for the downcast
the outcast
the unpitied
the unpenitent
that they should
turn their eyes
even from crosses
to his
Father-forgive-them
mortal majesty,
that they should,
in torture's grip
stumbling through
the dark valley
along the high hill,
still mutter
Jesus, remember me.

I must
remember
this and one
more thing
about this
strange person
whom some folk felt
constrained to call
a king:

I am
the thief
to whom
he listens
and replies.
I am
one of
the malefactors
for whom
he dies.

Luke 23:42

Better than Denial

Denial
is not always
visible
or audible.

The visible
appears permissible
even applaudable
at Jesus' trial
when he
is knocked
and struck
and mocked.

Caution
seems laudable

when our survival
is at stake.
We rival
Peter
and Pilate
and the soldiers
when we make
little
the large
of our disloyalty.

Better to be
a criminal
assigned
to die beside him
able to say —
to plead —
to pray
"Remember me."
Today!

Luke 23:42

Assignment

Is there anything
I can do
for you?
I politely
inquire
of my distressed
friends

fancying
the answer
is No.

Standing
by the cross
of Jesus
I conjecture
there is nothing
that can be
done
for his comfort
at this late
date
no last
request
he might address
to me.

Instead
he says
Behold
my mother
my sister
my brother
all yours.
Take care
of them
for me.

John 19:25-27

Why?

O God, why
have you swept me under
the carpet like dirt
interred in the least
remarkable manner?
Why, O God,
have you curbed my joy
and accelerated
my pain?
I am sick
and tired
in more ways
than two.
Is there a good reason
or did it just happen
while you were occupied
with other children's business?

Matthew 27:46
Mark 15:34

There Was Darkness Over the Whole Land

Looking back to heaven
he saw the sky was empty.
His cry reverberated
Why? and all he heard
was *Why?* . . .
My God . . .
and
Why?
echoing
without
an audible
reply.

His outstretched arms
his sunshot eyes
his mortal mouth
making the words
and taking them back
again:
Oh why? . . .
My God . . .
Oh why
am I
forsaken?

An orphan
crying
to himself
calling to
an unborn
father.

Or so it seemed
as the mob stared
and the stars
were nowhere
to be seen
or heard
and the cross shook —
and the world.

Matthew 27:46
Mark 15:34

My God

Despite all
appearances
to the contrary
God
blesses

Our curses
and questions
collapse
when we know Him
better

*My God
why hast Thou
forsaken me*
becomes
My God

There are
no tenderer
no stronger
words than
these

Matthew 27:46
Mark 15:34

Finishing Touch

He drove
the last
nail.
Not they
but he
finished
the uphill
work
executed
his own
life
enterprise
hung up
unbroken
bones
as well-worn
tools
to consummate
his handiwork
and achieve

his all-embracing
and complete
labor of love.

John 19:30

Into Your Hands

Your hand
your hands
protect me
safeguard me
for the preservation
of all that lasts
forever.

I transfer
by deed
and word
my trust
and my commitment.

Deliver
my soul
to your house.
Make my
last will
your will.

Luke 23:46

X

Near the city dump
they set the sign
of man's renewal
(his cities
and his soul).
X marks the spot.

Matthew 27:33-56
Mark 15:22-41
Luke 23:33-49
John 19:17-30

Scavenging Savior

Do not confuse
the clean new tomb
of Joseph's adjacent garden
with Golgotha's sanitary landfill
where the world's offal
found its disposal
before closing time
one Friday —
and yet their nearness
is no accident
and clearly appropriate
to God's gracious scavenging.

Unnailing Us

With his own nail-torn hands
he conquers
the torturous things
which nail us.

Matthew 27:33-56
Mark 15:22-41
Luke 23:33-49
John 19:17-30

BREATH OF LIFE

Breath of Life

What have we done with Jesus?
Have we laid him
outside the tomb,
outside our cognizance?
His resurrection —
in our specious thinking —
is a bare figment
of divine romance.
And yet he comes
back from the banishment
we try to force on him,
our death his death
in our malign
imagination. Yet in Easter's
twilight on us
he breathes his Spirit breath.

John 21:19-23 (especially v. 22)

To Be Continued

It happened . . .
and we catch
some moving
camera shots
some brief
recordings of
the sights
and sounds

odors
and fragrances
flavor
and savor
zest
and gusto
that touched
and changed
their world
and ours.
And we rejoice
we have
as many
glimpses
and memories
of acts
and words
which share
the certainty
and substance
of the constantly
to-be-continued
life and presence
of Jesus Christ
among us.

The Broken Silence

They broke their silence
when they gained their breath
after their flight
from the astounding garden.

Their articulation
of their experience,
their witness to the wonder
and the glory
was premise, preface, prelude
to the proclamation
of the cataclysmal
promise and power
of Jesus'
resurrection.

Mark 16:8

Resurrection Yarn

The resurrection yarn
was much too good
to be confounded with reality

Farfetched
trumped up
a fabrication

a fairy tale
mere idle women's gossip
not for a man's believing

and yet corroborated
by his witness
and by theirs.

Luke 24:11

Come

Jesus,
who wakened
on that Easter morning,
come, waken me.
Come, waken me.

Identification

The cadence of his voice
the nuance of her name
enabled Mary
to consummate
the resurrection
morning meeting
in the garden.

John 20:11-18

My Resurrection Too

I cannot bring myself
to choose to carry
a crossbeamed burden
or to welcome nails
in order to merit
(if merit is the word)
an Easter of my own.

And yet
and yet
I cannot quite
abandon
the hope of Easter.

If I believed it
I would run
like John
and Peter
through the morning.

I would exclaim
like Thomas
when I recognized
the telltale wounds
which guaranteed
the passion
of the person
he confronted
the presence
of a friend
much more than friend.

But still
like Peter
I would need to answer
his pertinent
recurrent question
Do you love me?
and not by words
alone.

And yet
I do.
I do.
I do.

Lord, overlook
the insouciance
the impotence
the arrogance
of my undoing
and my abstinence
from love
and lovingkindness.

Raise me up
so that your Easter
means my resurrection too.

Fulfill your promise
I am with you always.

Matthew 28
Mark 16
Luke 24
John 20

Under the Sign of Thomas

Under the sign of Thomas
we live — we doubters —
we wonderers — we wanderers —
scrupulously suspicious
of human and inhuman
dogmatisms
unfootnoted creeds
and facile suppositions.

We must put
our heads as well as our fingers
at the point where facts
puncture the flesh
and measure how far
love can unsafely go.

                                        John 20:24-27

Unless I See

After the vacuum of that endless week
with no promised Lord's Day waiting past its close,
despondent Thomas would not change his words
demanding wounds to show his Master rose
more than in minds desiring his return
with such a passion they could clothe the air
with the loved countenance. His dark suspense
would not suspend the deadness of his prayer.
Unless I see, Unless I see, he said —
and who will blame him the intensity
of his concern for certainty? He bled
to know the bloodmarks real. *Unless I see!*
And now the ten, reliving their surprise
when Life rejoined them in the quiet room,
turn all their eyes upon the singular
denier of the bare and canceled tomb
and hear the exclamation of assent,
the shout of faith alert and open-eyed:
My Lord! My God! And he who faces Christ
finds all his claims to fealty verified.

John 20:24-28

149

No Accident

We too are inspectors
of the resurrection.
We examine such evidence
as empty excavations
and guilty guards
provide for our appraisal.
We calculate the significance
of inhabited gardens
and startled confidants.

The relevance of revelation
waits on our manner
of handling the available,
our style of seeing,
our fingerprints of feeling,
until the decisive confession
is wrung from our confrontation.
It is no accident
we are called Thomas.

John 20:24-28

His Memoirs

If Jesus had written his memoirs we would prize
and venerate the book but would we bless
his paragraphs with daily faithfulness
or — like the Gospel — cut them down to size
to fit convenience? Would we choose to miss
the ardor and the passion as each phrase
detailed the spirit and intent his days
communicated? His hypothesis
of service we might lose in one bright blur,
preferring to be worshipper, not follower.

Luke 1:1-4

Unfinished Symphony

My life of Jesus
and my life with Jesus
will be — must be —
an unfinished symphony.
The latest notes
are not the last.

Thank God.

Our Omega

There are old endings
to the story —
as best they could
they tried to tie a knot
as though the gospel
might unravel
without their firm
conclusion.
Happily ever after
is less true and more.
There were no words
to catalyze their joy.
The Word Himself
has spoken no last word
as yet.
There is no ending.
He is our Omega.

Revelation 1:8; 21:6; 22:13

INDEX OF SCRIPTURE
REFERENCES

This index is only a partial index, but it will enable you to find many of the poems that fit the Scripture/Lectionary passages which you are studying or from which you are planning to preach.

Indispensable to this book is my earlier book entitled *Beginning with Mary*, which provides 132 poems on the life of Jesus from the very important standpoint of the women who had a part in it. I wanted to include these poems in this index, but the passages they are based on should be relatively easy to find without an index. A cursory reading of the Table of Contents will help you find what you want.

It would be best to supplement the entries here with your own notions of pertinent passages. I didn't give Scripture references for a number of the poems here because there were simply too many pertinent passages to list. But a good concordance will help you in this regard. From your own experience with poetry you might also want to add notations regarding the hundreds of poems that you know on Gospel themes by literally hundreds of authors.

To David Livingstone Harold Carlisle I am indebted for preparation of this index, a labor of care and love.